50 RECIPES FOR

FROMAGE FRAIS

Sainsbury's

Published exclusively for J Sainsbury plc
Stamford House   Stamford Street
London   SE1 9LL
by Martin Books
Simon & Schuster International Group
Fitzwilliam House   32 Trumpington Street
Cambridge CB2 1QY

First published 1989
Second impression 1989

Recipes by Robin Ayrdon
Design by Patrick McLeavey & Partners
Photography by The Food Studio
Food preparation for photography by Sandra Baddeley

Typesetting by Goodfellow & Egan, Cambridge
Origination by Repro (Cambridge) Ltd, Cambridge
Printed and bound in Great Britain by The Eagle Press, Blantyre

Notes
Ingredients are given in both metric and imperial quantities.
Use either set of quantities, but not a mixture of both, in
any one recipe.
All spoon measurements are in level spoons.
1 tablespoon = one 15 ml spoon; 1 teaspoon = one 5 ml spoon.
Fresh herbs are used unless otherwise stated.
Dried herbs can be substituted, but halve the quantities.
Eggs are standard (size three) unless otherwise stated.

Cover recipe: Strawberry Cheese Rings (page 54).

INTRODUCTION

Fromage frais is a delicious low-fat, very soft moist cheese which has a light, smooth texture and a mild, fresh, creamy taste. It is highly versatile and can be enjoyed on its own or as an ingredient in both sweet and savoury dishes. Its usefulness is shown in these recipes: it adds richness and creaminess to anything from soups to salads, such as the Baked Rice Salad on page 20, or sauces, such as in Honeyed Duck with Plums (page 44) or casseroles, such as Lemon Roast Lamb (page 36); and of course also to desserts, such as the Strawberry Cheese Rings (page 54), illustrated on the cover, or the Veiled Apple Pudding (page 58). Fromage frais has a spoonable consistency which makes it convenient.

Produced to a traditional French recipe, and made from pasteurised skimmed milk, fromage frais is made just like any other cheese. The difference is that it is fermented for only a very short time which is why the French call it 'frais', meaning fresh, and it should be eaten as fresh as possible.

Fromage frais has been eaten in France for decades, where the French use generous quantities in all kinds of tempting recipes, consuming some 400,000 tons of it every year. Since 1983, when it was first sold in Sainsbury's, it has become increasingly popular in Britain, too.

Sainsbury's 8% fat fromage frais has double cream added to it during manufacture, to give a rich creamy flavour. Even then, the 8% fat fromage frais contains less than half the fat of single cream.

The virtually fat-free fromage frais contains less than 1% fat, compared with double cream which contains 48% fat. It is the ideal choice if you are watching your diet, because it contains only 45 calories per 100 g. Use it whenever you would normally use cream, to spoon onto canned fruit or desserts, or mix with herbs, fresh or dried, and use as a topping for baked potatoes.

For everyone interested in their health and their cooking, fromage frais will soon become a regular item on the shopping list.

RECIPE FINDER

Recipes in this Recipe Finder are grouped in useful categories, so that you can quickly find the right dish for a particular meal.

All the recipes in this book are listed here, and many are included in more than one category.

ACCOMPANIMENTS

Carrot and leek rarebit 50
Courgettes with parsley sauce 46
Minty parcels 48
Parsnips with carrot sauce 50
Peas in tomato cream 47
Potato bake 52

CHICKEN, DUCK AND TURKEY DISHES

Cold chicken in walnut sauce 42
Creamy chicken tomatoes 12
Croissants with chicken filling 22
Honeyed duck with plums 44
Marmalade chicken 42
St Clement's salad 22
Turkey kebabs with peanut sauce 44

DESSERTS

Baked coffee custard 60
Bread and pineapple pudding 60
Coconut sponge 62
Fruit and nut fool 54
Layered apricot cheesecake 58
Moulded raspberry creams 56
Slimmers' chocolate mousse 56

Spiced pancakes 62
Strawberry cheese rings 54
Veiled apple pudding 58

FISH DISHES

Caribbean prawns 32
Haddock choux 30
Seafood gratin 16
Smoked haddock rolls 24
Stuffed plaice florentine 32
Trout with mustard sauce 30
Tuna toasts 26

LIGHT MEALS

Baked rice salad 20
Carrot and leek rarebit 50
Creamy chicken tomatoes 12
Croissants with chicken filling 22
Ham and broccoli au gratin 24
Kidney and mushroom toasts 26
Mediterranean salad 20
Mixed vegetable omelette 19
Nut crunch with fresh vegetable sticks 28
Seafood gratin 16
Smoked haddock rolls 24
St Clement's salad 22
Tuna toasts 26
Vegetable and pasta salad 29

MAIN MEALS

Caribbean prawns 32
Cheese-crusted pork chops 38
Cold chicken in walnut sauce 42

Devilled beef stir-fry 36
Haddock choux 30
Ham and apple sauté with pasta 34
Honeyed duck with plums 44
Lamb korma 38
Lemon roast lamb 36
Malay beef bake 40
Marmalade chicken 42
Peppered veal 34
Stuffed plaice florentine 32
Trout with mustard sauce 30
Turkey kebabs with peanut sauce 44
Watercress steak 40

MEAT DISHES

Cheese-crusted pork chops 38
Devilled beef stir-fry 36
Ham and apple sauté with pasta 34
Ham and broccoli au gratin 24
Kidney and mushroom toasts 26
Lamb korma 38
Lemon roast lamb 36
Malay beef bake 40
Peppered veal 34
Watercress steak 40

PASTA AND RICE DISHES

Baked rice salad 20
Ham and apple sauté with pasta 34
Vegetable and pasta salad 29

SALADS

Baked rice salad 20

Mediterranean salad 20
St Clement's salad 22
Vegetable and pasta salad 29

SOUPS AND STARTERS

Aubergine pâté 16
Beetroot soup 18
Cheese and vegetable soup 10
Cream of lettuce soup 8
Creamy chicken tomatoes 12
Creole-style tomato soup 12
Nut crunch with fresh vegetable sticks 28
Parsley and pepper mousse 14
Pears with tomato and tarragon 14
Pea soup with ham dumplings 8
Red and yellow stuffed eggs 11
Seafood gratin 16

MEATLESS SNACKS AND SUPPERS

Aubergine pâté 16
Baked rice salad 20
Broccoli soufflé 48
Carrot and leek rarebit 50
Courgettes with parsley sauce 46
Mediterranean salad 20
Minty parcels 48
Mixed vegetable omelette 19
Nut crunch with fresh vegetable sticks 28
Parsnips with carrot sauce 50
Pears with tomato and tarragon 14
Peas in tomato cream 47
Potato bake 52
Sweet pepper and olive flan 52
Vegetable and pasta salad 29

CREAM OF LETTUCE SOUP

SERVES 4–6

25 g (1 oz) butter
1 small onion, chopped
200 g (7 oz) lettuce leaves,
    shredded
450 ml (¾ pint) chicken stock
a good pinch of sugar
2 egg yolks, beaten
100 g (3 ½ oz) fromage frais
2 tablespoons flaked almonds,
    toasted
salt and pepper

1. Melt the butter in a saucepan and sauté the onion for 3 minutes.
2. Reserve a few shreds of lettuce and stir the rest into the pan. Pour on the stock, bring to the boil and simmer for 5 minutes.
3 Purée the soup and return to the pan. Stir in the sugar and seasoning. Add the egg yolks and stir over a moderate heat for 3 minutes. Cool for 5 minutes.
4. Blend the fromage frais into the soup and crumble in most of the almonds.
5. Serve hot or cold garnished with lettuce shreds and the remaining almonds.

NOTE:
This soup can also be made with spinach.
Freezing: not recommended

PEA SOUP WITH HAM DUMPLINGS

SERVES 4

475 g (15 oz) frozen peas
1 teaspoon sugar
900 ml (1½ pints) boiling water
125 g (4 oz) fromage frais
1 teaspoon cornflour
1 egg yolk
40 g (1½ oz) plain flour
2 tablespoons melted butter
25 g (1 oz) ham, shredded
salt and pepper

1. Simmer the peas with the sugar and water for 10–12 minutes, until soft. Purée and press through a sieve into a clean saucepan.
2. Blend half the fromage frais with the cornflour and stir into the soup. Season and place over a moderate heat.
3. Beat the egg yolk with the flour and remaining fromage frais. Gradually add the butter, ham and a pinch of salt.
4. Drop small spoonfuls of the batter into the gently simmering soup and cook for 8–10 minutes.
Freezing: not recommended

Top *Pea Soup with Ham Dumpling*, below *Cream of Lettuce Soup*

CHEESE AND VEGETABLE SOUP

SERVES 4

40 g (1½ oz) butter
150 g (5 oz) potatoes, diced
150 g (5 oz) courgettes, sliced
150 g (5 oz) leeks, sliced
150 g (5 oz) cauliflower florets
900 ml (1½ pints) chicken stock
6 tablespoons fromage frais
25 g (1 oz) Cheddar cheese,
    grated
salt and pepper

1. Melt the butter in a large saucepan. Add the vegetables and stir until coated. Cover and cook on a low heat for 5 minutes.
2. Pour the stock over the vegetables and bring to the boil. Cover and simmer for 15 minutes. Season to taste.
3. Combine the fromage frais and Cheddar.
4. Spoon the soup into warmed serving bowls and spoon on the cheese topping.
Freezing: not recommended

RED AND YELLOW STUFFED EGGS

SERVES 4

4 hard-boiled eggs
1 teaspoon grated onion
4 tablespoons fromage frais
½ teaspoon tomato purée
¼ teaspoon curry powder
salt and pepper
tomato slivers and watercress
  sprigs, to garnish

1. Shell and halve the eggs. Scoop the yolks into a basin, beat in the onion and fromage frais, and season.
2. Divide the mixture in two and stir the tomato purée into one half and the curry powder into the other.
3. Fill 4 egg whites with the tomato mixture and 4 with the curry mixture. Chill for 1 hour.
4. Garnish the red eggs with a sliver of tomato and the yellow ones with a sprig of watercress.
5. Arrange contrasting eggs on four serving plates and add a few more sprigs of watercress.
Freezing: not recommended

CREOLE-STYLE TOMATO SOUP

SERVES 4–6

25 g (1 oz) butter
1 small onion, chopped
1 medium-size red pepper, de-seeded and chopped
2 tablespoons plain flour
¼ teaspoon paprika
397 g (14 oz) can of chopped tomatoes
750 ml (1¼ pints) chicken stock
125 g (4 oz) 8% fat fromage frais
½ teaspoon grated orange zest

1. Melt the butter in a pan and gently cook the onion and pepper until soft. Blend in the flour and half the paprika and stir for 1 minute.
2. Increase the heat and stir in the tomatoes and the stock. Bring to the boil, cover and simmer for 20 minutes.
3. Purée the soup and return it to the pan.
4. Combine the fromage frais and orange zest and stir half into the soup. Re-heat without boiling.
5. Swirl the remaining fromage frais mixture into the soup just before serving and sprinkle with the remaining paprika.
Freezing: recommended after stage 4

CREAMY CHICKEN TOMATOES

SERVES 4

4 extra-large tomatoes
150 g (5 oz) cooked chicken, chopped
½ small onion, chopped
1 egg
1 tablespoon sweet pickle
6 tablespoons fromage frais
oil for greasing
salt and pepper

1. Preheat the oven to Gas Mark 6/200°C/400°F.
2. Put the tomatoes stalk-side down, and make 5 parallel cuts down through each one, leaving them joined at the base.
3. Put the chicken, onion, egg and pickle in a food processor and chop until fairly smooth. Blend in the fromage frais and seasoning.
4. Spoon the mixture between the tomato slices, and put in a greased, ovenproof dish.
5. Bake the tomatoes for 12–15 minutes, until just set. Serve hot, accompanied by triangles of toast.
Freezing: not recommended

Top *Creole-style Tomato Soup*, below *Creamy Chicken Tomatoes*

PARSLEY AND PEPPER MOUSSE

SERVES 4

2 large green peppers
2 tablespoons chopped parsley
25 g (1 oz) butter
11 g (0.4 oz) sachet of gelatine
6 tablespoons weak chicken stock
½ teaspoon caster sugar
200 g (7 oz) fromage frais
salt and pepper

1. Pare the skin from the peppers with a potato peeler. Slice the flesh, discarding the cores and seeds.
2. Reserve 12 pieces of pepper to garnish, and gently cook the remainder with the parsley in the butter over a low heat for 8–10 minutes until soft.
3. Dissolve the gelatine in 3 tablespoons of the stock.
4. Purée the peppers and parsley with the sugar and remaining stock, gradually blending in the gelatine liquid.
5. Fold the fromage frais into the pepper purée and season. Pour into individual soufflé dishes, moulds or cut down yogurt pots and chill until set.
6. Unmould the mousses onto small plates. Garnish with the reserved pepper.
Freezing: not recommended

PEARS WITH TOMATO AND TARRAGON

SERVES 4

2 large dessert pears
175 g (6 oz) fromage frais
1 tablespoon white wine vinegar
½ teaspoon dried tarragon
¼ teaspoon caster sugar
1 teaspoon tomato purée
¼ teaspoon paprika
salt and pepper
tomato slices, to garnish

1. Peel and halve the pears. Scoop out the cores with a teaspoon and place the fruit on serving plates.
2. Lightly beat the fromage frais with the vinegar, tarragon, sugar and tomato purée. Season with salt and pepper.
3. Spoon the dressing over the pears, completely covering them. Chill for 30 minutes.
4. Sprinkle the pears with paprika before serving and add tomato slices to the plates.
Freezing: not recommended

Top *Parsley and Pepper Mousse,* below *Pears with Tomato and Tarragon*

SEAFOOD GRATIN

SERVES 4

250 g (8 oz) cod fillets, skinned
25 g (1 oz) butter
4 spring onions, chopped
50 g (2 oz) peeled prawns
2 egg yolks
1 teaspoon cornflour
200 g (7 oz) fromage frais
1 tablespoon chopped parsley
1 tablespoon grated parmesan
    cheese
salt and pepper

1. Cut the cod into chunks.
2. Melt the butter in a pan over a low heat and use a little to coat the inside of 1 large or 4 small flameproof dishes. Scallop shells can be used, if available.
3. Gently fry the cod and spring onions in the remaining butter for 3–4 minutes. Add the prawns and spoon into the prepared dishes.
4. Preheat the grill to moderately hot.
5. Combine the egg yolks, cornflour, fromage frais and parsley. Spoon over the fish and season. Sprinkle on the parmesan and grill for 4–5 minutes until well browned.
Freezing: not recommended

AUBERGINE PÂTÉ

SERVES 4–6

1 large aubergine
2 tablespoons olive oil
1 garlic clove, crushed
1 tablespoon chopped parsley
¼ teaspoon ground cumin
100 g (3½ oz) fromage frais
salt and pepper

1. Preheat the grill to hot.
2. Coat the aubergine with a film of oil and grill for 12–15 minutes until soft and pulpy, turning once during cooking.
3. Halve the aubergine and scoop the flesh into a liquidiser. With the machine running, beat in the oil and garlic.
4. Turn the purée into a bowl and fold in the chopped parsley, cumin, fromage frais and seasoning.
5. Chill the pâté for 1 hour. Serve with toast or sliced pitta bread.
Freezing: not recommended

Top *Aubergine Pâté*, below
Seafood Gratin

BEETROOT SOUP

SERVES 4

425 g (14 oz) cooked beetroot,
    coarsely grated
½ large onion, chopped
1 litre (1¾ pints) beef stock
2 teaspoons lemon juice
2 tablespoons dry sherry
    (optional)
1½ tablespoons chopped chives
6 tablespoons fromage frais
salt and pepper

1. Put the beetroot, onion and stock in a saucepan and bring to the boil. Cover and simmer for 20 minutes.
2. Strain the beetroot liquid into a clean pan. Add the lemon juice, sherry and seasoning and reheat for 2–3 minutes.
3. If serving cold, cool the soup and then chill until required.
3. Pour the soup into bowls and add a little of the cooked, grated beetroot.
4. Fold the chives into the fromage frais and add a spoonful to each bowl before serving hot or cold.
Freezing: recommended after stage 2

MIXED VEGETABLE OMELETTE

SERVES 4–5

25 g (1 oz) butter
2 teaspoons vegetable oil
2 leeks, sliced
2 courgettes, sliced
2 tomatoes, chopped
2 tablespoons frozen peas
5 eggs, beaten
100 g (3½ oz) fromage frais
¼ teaspoon dried marjoram
salt and pepper

1. Melt the butter with the oil in a large frying-pan. Cook the leeks and courgettes on a low heat for 3–4 minutes, until softened.
2. Stir the tomatoes and peas into the pan and cook for 3 more minutes.
3. Combine the eggs, fromage frais, marjoram and seasoning and pour over the vegetables.
4. Cook the omelette over a moderate heat until just set, about 4–5 minutes. Cut into wedges and serve hot with a salad.
Freezing: not recommended

MEDITERRANEAN SALAD

SERVES 4

2 medium-size aubergines, cubed
1 tablespoon salt
1½ tablespoons olive oil
1 garlic clove, crushed
6 tomatoes, cut in wedges
12 black olives, halved and
   stoned
4 anchovy fillets, diced
2 teaspoons white wine vinegar
125 g (4 oz) fromage frais
½ teaspoon dried basil

1. Place the aubergines in a colander, sprinkle with the salt and leave for 30 minutes. Rinse well and dry on kitchen paper.
2. Heat the oil in a pan and fry the garlic and aubergine over a moderate heat until golden. Tip into a bowl.
3. Add the tomatoes and olives to the aubergines and stir in 3 of the diced anchovy fillets.
4. Pound the remaining anchovy fillet to a paste with the vinegar. Blend in the fromage frais and basil and stir into the salad. Cover and leave to stand for 1 hour.
Freezing: not recommended

BAKED RICE SALAD

SERVES 4–6

40 g (1½ oz) butter
1 onion, chopped
1 teaspoon curry powder
200 g (7 oz) long-grain rice
50 g (2 oz) blanched almonds,
   slivered
75 g (3 oz) red lentils
75 g (3 oz) currants
75 g (3 oz) dried apricots, slivered
575 ml (18 fl oz) chicken or
   vegetable stock
6 tablespoons fromage frais

1. Preheat the oven to Gas Mark 5/190°C/375°F.
2. Melt the butter in a pan and gently fry the onion until soft. Add the curry powder, rice and almonds and stir for 1 minute.
3. Turn the rice mixture into an ovenproof dish. Stir in the lentils and dried fruit and pour on the stock.
4. Cover the dish and bake for 40 minutes. Lightly fork the fromage frais into the salad and serve hot.
Freezing: not recommended

Top *Mediterranean Salad*, below *Baked Rice Salad*

ST CLEMENT'S SALAD

SERVES 4

1 medium-size red pepper, de-
  seeded and sliced
1 large orange
1 lemon
400 g (13 oz) cooked chicken,
  sliced
6 spring onions, sliced thickly
200 g (7 oz) fromage frais
1 tablespoon clear honey

1. Blanch the red pepper in boiling
water for 2 minutes. Drain, rinse
under cold water and leave to cool.
2. Shred thin curls of zest from the
orange and lemon. Put in a dish
with the chicken and spring onions.
Add the red pepper.
3. Peel the orange, cut the flesh
into wedges and add to the salad,
with any juice.
4. Squeeze the juice from the
lemon.
5. Whisk the fromage frais with the
honey and gradually add the lemon
juice. Stir into the salad, cover and
chill for 1 hour.
Freezing: not recommended

CROISSANTS WITH CHICKEN FILLING

SERVES 4

4 croissants, or soft rolls
40 g (1½ oz) butter
2 bacon rashers, chopped
75 g (3 oz) mushrooms, thinly
  sliced
2 tablespoons plain flour
150 ml (¼ pint) milk
125 g (4 oz) cooked chicken, diced
6 tablespoons fromage frais
salt and pepper

1. Preheat the oven to Gas Mark
2/150°C/300°F. Set the croissants
to warm through.
2. Melt the butter in a pan. Add the
bacon and mushrooms and fry
gently for 3 minutes, turning
occasionally.
3. Blend the flour into the bacon
mixture and stir for 1 minute.
Gradually blend in the milk, increase
the heat and stir until the sauce is
thick and smooth.
4. Reduce the heat and stir in the
chicken and fromage frais. Season.
5. Split open the the warmed
croissants or rolls, spoon in the
filling and serve immediately.
Freezing: not recommended

Top *St Clement's Salad*, below
Croissants with Chicken Filling

SMOKED HADDOCK ROLLS

SERVES 4

200 g (7 oz) smoked haddock fillet
4 spinach or lettuce leaves
4 round crisp bread rolls
25 g (1 oz) butter
4 spring onions, thinly sliced
1 tablespoon plain flour
6 tablespoons fromage frais
1 egg
a good pinch of ground nutmeg

---

1. Poach the haddock in simmering water for 5–6 minutes. Cool and flake the flesh. Soften the spinach or lettuce in boiling water for 1–2 minutes and pat dry.
2. Cut the tops from the rolls and scoop out the soft centres. Line the cavities with spinach.
3. Preheat the oven to Gas Mark 4/180°C/350°F.
4. Melt the butter and fry the onions for 1 minute. Blend in the flour and stir for 1 minute.
5. Beat the fromage frais with the egg and nutmeg. Add to the pan and stir for 2 minutes. Stir in the fish and remove from the heat.
6. Spoon the haddock mixture into the rolls. Replace the lids and wrap in foil.
7. Bake the rolls for 15 minutes and serve hot.

Freezing: recommended after stage 6

HAM AND BROCCOLI AU GRATIN

SERVES 4

175 g (6 oz) trimmed broccoli
½ teaspoon French mustard
4 slices of cooked ham
oil for greasing
150 g (5 oz) fromage frais
1 egg
2 tablespoons fresh breadcrumbs
25 g (1 oz) Cheddar cheese, grated
salt and pepper

---

1. Cut the broccoli into spears and cook in boiling, salted water for 3 minutes. Drain well.
2. Preheat the grill to hot.
3. Smear a little mustard onto each slice of ham. Arrange the broccoli along one edge of each and roll the slices up firmly. Put, join-sides down, in a greased, flameproof dish.
4. Beat the fromage frais with the egg and seasoning. Stir in the breadcrumbs and spoon over the ham rolls.
5. Sprinkle the grated cheese over the sauce and place the dish under the grill. Cook until brown and bubbling.

Freezing: not recommended

Top *Smoked Haddock Rolls*, below *Ham and Broccoli au Gratin*

KIDNEY AND MUSHROOM TOASTS

SERVES 4

4 lamb's kidneys
25 g (1 oz) butter
1 small onion, chopped
75 g (3 oz) green beans, sliced
   thickly
40 g (1½ oz) mushrooms, sliced
¼ teaspoon dried mixed herbs
2 tablespoons dry sherry
200 g (7 oz) fromage frais
1 tablespoon cornflour
1 teaspoon tomato purée
salt and pepper

1. Skin, halve and core the kidneys. Cut into thick slices.
2. Melt the butter in a pan over a moderate heat and fry the kidneys and onion for 2 minutes, stirring.
3. Stir in the beans, mushrooms and herbs. Pour on the sherry; cover and cook on a low heat for 5 minutes.
4. Combine the fromage frais, cornflour, tomato purée and seasoning. Add to the pan, increase the heat and stir until the sauce thickens.
5. Serve on toast or in split pitta breads.
Freezing: recommended

TUNA TOASTS

SERVES 4

25 g (1 oz) butter
½ small onion, chopped
1 stick of celery, chopped
1½ tablespoons plain flour
175 ml (6 fl oz) chicken stock
198 g (7 oz) can of tuna, drained
   and flaked
50 g (2 oz) gherkins, chopped
1 teaspoon English mustard
100 g (3 ½ oz) fromage frais
4 slices of hot toast

1. Melt the butter in a pan on a low heat and gently fry the onion and celery for 2 minutes.
2. Sprinkle the flour over the vegetables, and cook, stirring, for 1 minute. Gradually blend in the stock and bring to the boil, stirring constantly. Remove from the heat.
3. Stir the tuna, gherkins and mustard into the fromage frais and add to the vegetable sauce. Stir over a moderate heat for 4–5 minutes until hot.
4. Spread the creamed tuna on hot toast.
Freezing: not recommended

Top *Kidney and Mushroom Toasts*, below *Tuna Toasts*

NUT CRUNCH WITH FRESH VEGETABLE STICKS

SERVES 4–6

1 bulb of fennel
8 large radishes
4 carrots
4 sticks of celery
300 g (10 oz) fromage frais
113 g (4 oz) carton of cottage cheese

50 g (2 oz) hazelnut kernels, chopped
1 dessert apple

1. Slice the fennel and radishes and cut the carrots and celery into sticks. Chill for 15 minutes, to crispen them.
2. Lightly stir the fromage frais into the cottage cheese; then fold in the nuts.
3. Peel the apple and coarsely grate the flesh into the cheese mixture.
4. Arrange on serving plates.
Freezing: not recommended

VEGETABLE AND PASTA SALAD

SERVES 4–6

125 g (4 oz) pasta shells
200 g (7 oz) cauliflower florets
150 g (5 oz) broccoli florets
2 carrots, cut into matchsticks
25 g (1 oz) Danish blue cheese, crumbled
25 g (1 oz) butter
½ teaspoon cornflour
125 g (4 oz) fromage frais
213 g (4 ½ oz) can of red kidney beans, drained

1. Cook the pasta in boiling salted water for 4 minutes. Add the cauliflower, broccoli and carrots and cook for 4 more minutes. Drain and keep warm.
2. Return the pan to a low heat and in it stir the cheese and butter until melted. Blend in the cornflour and fromage frais.
3. Add the drained kidney beans and the pasta and hot vegetables to the sauce and cook on a low heat for 2–3 minutes. Serve hot.
Freezing: not recommended

HADDOCK CHOUX

SERVES 4

150 ml (¼ pint) water
65 g (2½ oz) butter, plus extra for greasing
65 g (2½ oz) plain flour, sifted, plus 2 tablespoons
2 eggs, beaten
50 g (2 oz) Cheddar cheese, grated
1 small onion, chopped
200 ml (7 fl oz) chicken stock
300 g (10 oz) skinless haddock fillets, cut into chunks
125 g (4 oz) broccoli florets
100 g (3½ oz) fromage frais
salt and pepper

1. Preheat the oven to Gas Mark 6/200°C/400°F.
2. Bring the water and 50 g (2 oz) of the butter to the boil. Tip in the 65 g (2½ oz) of flour and beat well. Beat in the eggs and cheese and spoon in a narrow border around a greased ovenproof dish.
3. Melt the remaining butter and gently fry the onion for 2 minutes. Sprinkle on the remaining 2 tablespoons of flour and blend in the stock. Stir until thick and smooth.
4. Fold the haddock, broccoli and fromage frais into the sauce. Season and spoon into the centre of the dish. Bake for 35–40 minutes and serve hot.
Freezing: not recommended

TROUT WITH MUSTARD SAUCE

SERVES 4

4 x 250 g (8 oz) rainbow trout, cleaned
25 g (1 oz) butter
1 garlic clove, crushed
1 tablespoon plain flour
250 g (8 oz) fromage frais
2 teaspoons French mustard
2 tablespoons milk
¼ teaspoon caster sugar
1 teaspoon lemon juice
salt and pepper

1. Preheat the grill to hot.
2. Wash the trout, pat dry and sprinkle seasoning into the cavities. Grill for 12–15 minutes, turning once.
3. Meanwhile, melt the butter in a pan over a moderate heat and fry the garlic for 2 minutes. Add the flour and stir for 1 minute.
4. Remove the pan from the heat and blend in the fromage frais, mustard, milk and sugar. Stir over a low heat until thick and smooth.
5. Stir the lemon juice into the sauce, before serving with the trout.
Freezing: not recommended

Top *Trout with Mustard Sauce*, below *Haddock Choux*

CARIBBEAN PRAWNS

SERVES 4

25 g (1 oz) butter
1 large garlic clove, crushed
1 medium-size onion, chopped
1 large green pepper, de-seeded and diced
4 courgettes, sliced
397 g (14 oz) can of chopped tomatoes
4 slices of wholemeal bread
200 g (7 oz) peeled prawns
200 g (7 oz) fromage frais
50 g (2 oz) Cheddar cheese, grated

1. Melt the butter in a saucepan over a low heat and fry the garlic, onion and green pepper for 3 minutes.
2. Stir in the courgettes and the tomatoes. Cover and simmer for 7 minutes.
3. Preheat the grill to hot.
4. Make one slice of bread into crumbs. Toast the remainder and cut each into four squares.
5. Stir the prawns into the tomato mixture and turn into a flameproof dish.
6. Combine the fromage frais, grated cheese and breadcrumbs and spread on the toasts. Float them on the prawn mixture and grill until the topping is bubbling.
Freezing: not recommended

STUFFED PLAICE FLORENTINE

SERVES 4

227 g (8 oz) packet of finely chopped frozen spinach, thawed
250 g (8 oz) fromage frais
6 tablespoons fresh breadcrumbs
½ small onion, chopped
1 egg yolk
4 x 125 g (4 oz) plaice fillets
2 teaspoons lemon juice
2 teaspoons cornflour
salt and pepper

1. Preheat the oven to Gas Mark 5/190°C/375°F.
2. Stir 150 g (5 oz) of the fromage frais into half the spinach, and add the breadcrumbs, onion, seasoning and the egg yolk.
3. Lay the plaice skin-side up, and spoon on the spinach mixture. Roll up the fillets and place in an ovenproof dish. Sprinkle with lemon juice, cover and bake for 20–25 minutes.
4. Beat the remaining fromage frais with the cornflour. Add to the spinach in the pan and stir over a moderate heat until thickened. Serve with the fish.
Freezing: not recommended

Top *Stuffed Plaice Florentine*, below *Caribbean Prawns*

PEPPERED VEAL

SERVES 4

4 veal escalopes
2 teaspoons black peppercorns,
   crushed
25 g (1 oz) butter
1 medium-size green pepper, de-
   seeded and sliced
50 g (2 oz) mushrooms, sliced
½ teaspoon dried marjoram
½ teaspoon brown sugar
175 ml (6 fl oz) dry white wine or
   weak chicken stock
150 g (5 oz) 8% fat fromage frais

1. Cut the escalopes in two and rub
with the peppercorns.
2. Melt three-quarters of the butter
in a pan and fry the veal on a fairly
high heat for 3 minutes on each
side. Remove with a slotted spoon
and keep warm.
3. Add the green pepper and
mushrooms to the pan, with the
remaining butter. Stir until coated,
then add the marjoram, sugar and
wine or stock.
4. Increase the heat and cook until
the liquid is reduced by half, about
4–5 minutes.
5. Reduce the heat to low and blend
in the fromage frais. Return the veal
and any juices to the pan and reheat, without boiling.
Freezing: not recommended

HAM AND APPLE SAUTÉ WITH PASTA

SERVES 4–5

250 g (8 oz) tagliatelle verdi
25 g (1 oz) butter
6 spring onions, sliced
1 dessert apple, peeled, cored
   and diced
200 g (7 oz) prime ham steaks,
   diced
1 tablespoon plain flour
¼ teaspoon dried sage
4 tablespoons apple juice
1 egg
100 g (3½ oz) fromage frais

1. Put the tagliatelle to cook in
salted, boiling water, according to
the pack instructions.
2. Melt the butter in a pan over a
low heat and stir-fry the spring
onions, apple and ham for 2–3
minutes, until the apple softens.
3. Sprinkle on the flour and sage
and blend in the apple juice. Stir
until thick.
4. Beat the egg with the fromage
frais and stir into the pan. Cook
gently for 3–4 minutes until the
sauce thickens.
5. Drain the pasta, and serve with
the ham and apple mixture.
Freezing: not recommended

Top *Ham and Apple Sauté with
Pasta*, below *Peppered Veal*

DEVILLED BEEF STIR-FRY

SERVES 4

½ small onion, chopped finely
1 tablespoon tomato purée
2 teaspoons French mustard
2 teaspoons Worcestershire sauce
1 teaspoon lemon juice
1 teaspoon brown sugar
¼ teaspoon chilli powder
200 g (7 oz) fromage frais
475 g (15 oz) lean quick-grill steak
1 tablespoon olive oil
salt and pepper

1. Stir the onion, tomato purée, mustard, Worcestershire sauce, lemon juice, sugar, chilli powder and seasoning into the fromage frais and stand for 15 minutes for the flavours to develop.
2. Cut the beef into long thin strips and pat off excess moisture with kitchen paper.
3. Heat the oil in a pan and quickly stir-fry the beef over a high heat until browned all over.
4. Reduce the heat and stir the devil sauce into the beef. Cook gently for 3–4 minutes and serve immediately with rice or crisp vegetables.
Freezing: not recommended

LEMON ROAST LAMB

SERVES 6

1 kg (2 lb) boneless half-shoulder of lamb
1 sprig of rosemary, crumbled
1 garlic clove, slivered
grated zest and juice of 1 lemon
175 ml (6 fl oz) dry white wine
1 tablespoon cornflour
½ teaspoon caster sugar
125 g (4 oz) fromage frais
salt and pepper

1. Preheat the oven to Gas Mark 6/200°C/400°F.
2. Cut slits in the lamb and insert the rosemary and garlic. Rub on seasoning.
3. Put the lamb in a roasting dish or tin and sprinkle with the lemon zest and juice. Pour on the wine and roast for 25 minutes.
4. Reduce the temperature to Gas Mark 4/180°C/350°F and cook for 50–60 more minutes. Transfer to a dish and keep warm.
5. Strain the cooking liquids into a pan. Blend the cornflour with the sugar, add the fromage frais and stir into the cooking juices. Stir until thickened, and serve with the lamb.
Freezing: not recommended

Top *Devilled Beef Stir-fry*, below *Lemon Roast Lamb*

LAMB KORMA

SERVES 4

500 g (1 lb) lamb neck fillet, cubed
2.5 cm (1-inch) piece of fresh
    ginger, peeled and grated
1 garlic clove, crushed
2 teaspoons tomato purée
1 teaspoon.salt
1 teaspoon ground coriander
1 tablespoon mild curry powder
400 g (13 oz) fromage frais
1 onion, chopped
2 tablespoons vegetable oil
25 g (1 oz) ground almonds

1. Put the lamb in a shallow dish. Blend the ginger, garlic, tomato purée, salt and spices to a paste, with half the fromage frais and 1 tablespoon of onion. Stir into the lamb and leave to stand for 1 hour.
2. Heat the oil in a pan and fry the remaining onion until golden. Add the meat, a little at a time, and fry to seal all over. Stir in the remaining marinade, cover and cook on a low heat for 20 minutes.
3. Blend the remaining fromage frais with the ground almonds and stir into the lamb.
4. Cook the lamb on a low heat for 1 hour more, adding a little water as necessary. Serve with rice.
Freezing: recommended

CHEESE-CRUSTED PORK CHOPS

SERVES 4

½ teaspoon mustard
1 teaspoon dried sage
4 boneless pork loin chops
25 g (1 oz) butter
125 ml (4 fl oz) apple juice
125 g (4 oz) fromage frais
½ teaspoon cornflour
3 tablespoons fresh breadcrumbs
1½ tablespoons grated
    parmesan cheese
salt and pepper

1. Combine half the mustard with the sage and seasoning and brush over the chops.
2. Melt the butter in a pan over a moderate heat and brown the chops on both sides. Pour on the apple juice; cover and cook on a low heat for 25–30 minutes.
3. Preheat the grill to hot.
4. Beat the fromage frais with the cornflour and remaining mustard. Stir in the breadcrumbs and parmesan cheese and spread over the chops.
5. Grill the chops for 2–3 minutes, until the topping is well browned.
Freezing: not recommended

Top *Lamb Korma*, below *Cheese-crusted Pork Chops*

WATERCRESS STEAK

SERVES 4

1 bunch of watercress, trimmed
40 g (1½ oz) butter
½ small onion, chopped
1 teaspoon capers, chopped
2 tablespoons dry white wine or
   wine vinegar
4 rump or sirloin steaks
1½ teaspoons vegetable oil
200 g (7 oz) 8% fat fromage frais
1 teaspoon cornflour
a pinch of caster sugar
salt and pepper

1. Preheat the grill to very hot.
2. Reserve a few sprigs of watercress for garnish, and finely chop the remainder.
3. Melt the butter in a pan and gently cook the onion for 2 minutes. Stir in the watercress and capers. Pour on the wine, cover and cook on a low heat for 3–4 minutes.
4. Brush the steaks with oil and sprinkle with pepper. Cook for 2–3 minutes on each side for rare steaks, 4–5 minutes for medium and 6–7 minutes for well-done steaks.
5. Meanwhile beat the fromage frais with the cornflour and sugar. Stir into the watercress mixture and cook on a low heat. Season and serve with the steaks.
Freezing: not recommended

MALAY BEEF BAKE

SERVES 4–6

2 slices of bread
125 ml (4 fl oz) milk
500 g (1 lb) lean minced beef
1 onion, chopped
1 garlic clove, crushed
½ teaspoon turmeric
1½ teaspoons curry powder
50 g (2 oz) seedless raisins
25 g (1 oz) chopped almonds
1½ tablespoons lemon juice
2 eggs
100 g (3½ oz) fromage frais

1. Soak the bread in the milk.
2. Preheat the oven to Gas Mark 4/180°C/350°F.
3. In a large saucepan, brown the beef in its own fat. Add the onion, garlic, turmeric and curry powder and cook for 3 minutes. Remove from the heat and stir in the raisins, almonds and lemon juice.
4. Squeeze out the bread, and reserve the milk. Mash the bread into the beef. Pack the mixture into an ovenproof dish and bake for 45 minutes.
5. Beat the eggs with the fromage frais and a little of the reserved milk. Pour over the beef and bake for 30 more minutes.
Freezing: recommended

Top *Watercress Steak*, below
Malay Beef Bake

MARMALADE CHICKEN

SERVES 4

1½ tablespoons vegetable oil
4 part-boned chicken breasts
3 tablespoons orange juice
½ small onion, chopped
1½ tablespoons plain flour
2 tablespoons orange marmalade
200 g (7 oz) 8% fat fromage frais
1 egg yolk
salt and pepper

1. Preheat the oven to Gas Mark 4/180°C/350°F.
2. Heat half the oil in a pan on a moderate heat and brown the chicken breasts, skin-side down. Turn and seal the other side.
3. Transfer the chicken to a casserole and pour on the orange juice. Add seasoning, cover and bake for 45 minutes.
4. Heat the remaining oil in a pan on a low heat and fry the onion for 2 minutes. Add the flour and stir for 1 minute. Blend in the marmalade, fromage frais and egg yolk.
5. Drain the cooking liquids from the chicken and blend them into the marmalade sauce. Spoon the sauce over the chicken and bake for 15 more minutes.
Freezing: recommended

COLD CHICKEN IN WALNUT SAUCE

SERVES 4

4 chicken breast fillets
2 tablespoons orange juice
400 ml (14 fl oz) chicken stock
75 g (3 oz) walnut pieces
1 garlic clove, crushed
2 tablespoons brown
    breadcrumbs
a good pinch of chilli powder
300 g (10 oz) fromage frais

1. Put the chicken in a pan and pour on the orange juice and stock. Cover and poach on a moderate heat for 15–20 minutes. Leave to cool.
2. Meanwhile, reserve a few large walnut pieces and put the rest in a liquidiser with the garlic, breadcrumbs and chilli powder. Process to a coarse paste, slowly adding the fromage frais.
3. With a slotted spoon, or fish slice, transfer the chicken to a serving dish and add a little of the poaching liquid to the walnut sauce.
4. Spoon the sauce over the warm chicken. Add the reserved walnuts and leave until cold.
Freezing: not recommended

Top *Cold Chicken in Walnut Sauce*, below *Marmalade Chicken*

HONEYED DUCK WITH PLUMS

SERVES 4

4 duckling breast fillets
15 g (½ oz) butter
1 tablespoon clear honey
570 g (1 lb 3 oz) can of golden plums in light syrup
½ chicken stock cube, crumbled
1 ½ teaspoons cornflour
150 g (5 oz) fromage frais
salt and pepper

1. Preheat the oven to Gas Mark 7/220°C/425°F.
2. Score the duck skin. Melt the butter in a pan on a fairly high heat and quickly seal the duck on both sides.
3. Brush the duck all over with half the honey and put on a rack over a roasting pan. Roast for 18–20 minutes.
4. Reserve two of the plums and put the remainder in a saucepan with the syrup and the stock cube. Bring to the boil, remove stones with a fork, and purée with the cooking liquid.
5. Blend the remaining honey with the cornflour and fromage frais. Add to the plum purée and stir over moderate heat for 2–3 minutes.
6. Slice the duck and add half a plum to each serving with a little of the sauce.
Freezing: not recommended

TURKEY KEBABS WITH PEANUT SAUCE

SERVES 4–6

4 skinless turkey breast fillets, cubed
400 g (13 oz) fromage frais
1½ tablespoons lemon juice
2 tablespoons peanut butter
2 teaspoons soy sauce
2 teaspoons grated fresh ginger
2 teaspoons ground coriander
½ small onion, chopped
2 lemons, sliced

1. Put the turkey in a basin.
2. Beat the fromage frais with the lemon juice, peanut butter, and soy sauce, until smooth. Add the ginger, coriander and onion.
3. Stir the fromage frais mixture into the turkey; cover and refrigerate overnight.
4. Preheat the grill to hot.
5. Halve the lemon slices and discard any pips. Thread onto skewers, with the turkey.
6. Coat with marinade, where necessary, and cook 5 cm (2 inches) below the grill for 10 minutes. Turn, add more marinade, and grill for 8–10 minutes more.
Freezing: not recommended

Top *Turkey Kebabs with Peanut Sauce*, below *Honeyed Duck with Plums*

COURGETTES WITH PARSLEY SAUCE

SERVES 4–6

500 g (1 lb) courgettes, sliced
1 slice of lemon
25 g (1 oz) butter
½ small onion, chopped
4 tablespoons chopped fresh
   parsley
1 tablespoon plain flour
150 g (5 oz) fromage frais
a pinch of sugar
salt and pepper

1. Bring a pan of water to the boil and simmer the courgettes with the lemon slice for 2–3 minutes. Drain well and discard the lemon.
2. Melt the butter in the pan over a low heat and stir-fry the onion and parsley for 2 minutes. Blend in the flour and stir for 1 minute.
3. Return the courgettes to the pan and gradually blend in the fromage frais, sugar and seasoning. Reheat without boiling. Serve hot.
Freezing: not recommended

PEAS IN TOMATO CREAM

SERVES 4

25 g (1 oz) butter
1 teaspoon olive oil
½ small onion, chopped
1 clove garlic, crushed
250 g (8 oz) tomatoes
1½ teaspoons cornflour
1 teaspoon tomato purée
100 g (3½ oz) fromage frais
250 g (8 oz) fresh or frozen peas
salt and pepper

1. Melt the butter with the oil in a pan and gently fry the onion and garlic for 2 minutes.
2. Peel the tomatoes by immersing them in boiling water for 15 seconds, cooling under cold water, then skinning them. Slice them, then add to the pan. Cover and cook for 2 minutes.
3. Meanwhile, blend the cornflour with the tomato purée, fromage frais and seasoning.
4. Add the peas and fromage frais mixture to the pan. Cover and simmer on a low heat for 3–4 minutes for frozen peas and 8–10 minutes for fresh peas. Serve hot.
Freezing: not recommended

BROCCOLI SOUFFLÉ

SERVES 4

250 g (8 oz) broccoli, chopped
25 g (1 oz) butter
1 small onion, chopped
50 g (2 oz) mushrooms, chopped
3 tablespoons plain flour
100 ml (3½ fl oz) chicken or
   vegetable stock
3 eggs, separated
125 g (4 oz) fromage frais
1 teaspoon grated parmesan
   cheese
salt and pepper

1. Preheat the oven to Gas Mark
5/190°C/375°F.
2. Cook the broccoli in boiling water
for 3 minutes. Drain well.
3. Melt the butter in a pan over a
low heat and cook the onion and
mushrooms for 3 minutes. Blend in
the flour and stir for 1 minute.
4. Gradually add the stock to the
pan, increase the heat and stir until
the sauce is thick and smooth.
5. Remove the pan from the heat
and beat in the egg yolks and
fromage frais. Season to taste.
6. Whisk the egg whites until stiff.
Fold into the mixture, with the
broccoli. Turn into a greased 1–litre
(1¾-pint) soufflé dish, sprinkle with
the grated parmesan and bake for
35–40 minutes. Do not open the
oven door while the soufflé is
cooking. Serve immediately.
Freezing: not recommended

MINTY PARCELS

SERVES 4–6

300 g (10 oz) cauliflower florets
300 ml (½ pint) hot light stock
8 chinese leaves, trimmed
25 g (1 oz) butter
1 tablespoon chopped fresh mint
1 tablespoon plain flour
100 g (3½ oz) fromage frais
1 egg yolk
salt and pepper

1. Simmer the cauliflower in the
stock for 4–5 minutes. Drain and
reserve the stock.
2. Soften the chinese leaves in
boiling water for 2–3 minutes. Drain
and pat dry.
3. Melt the butter over a low heat,
stir in the mint and flour and cook
for 1 minute. Add 125 ml (4 fl oz) of
the reserved stock, increase the
heat and stir until thick.
4. Beat the fromage frais with the
egg yolk and seasoning. Stir into
the sauce, add the cauliflower and
cook on a low heat for 3–4 minutes.
5. Spoon the mixture onto the
chinese leaves and roll up. Reheat
in the oven at Gas Mark
5/190°/375°F for 10–15 minutes.
Freezing: not recommended

Top *Minty Parcels*, below *Broccoli
Soufflé*

CARROT AND LEEK RAREBIT

SERVES 4

575 ml (18 fl oz) beef or vegetable
 stock
500 g (1 lb) carrots, sliced
250 g (8 oz) trimmed leeks
½ teaspoon dried thyme
400 g (13 oz) fromage frais
¼ teaspoon made mustard
a pinch of sugar
2 tablespoons fresh breadcrumbs
50 g (2 oz) Double Gloucester
 cheese, grated finely
salt and pepper

1. Bring the stock to the boil in a
pan. Add the carrots and leeks,
cover and simmer for 8–10
minutes, until barely tender. Drain
well, reserving the stock.
2. Place the vegetables in a
shallow, flameproof dish and
sprinkle with thyme and seasoning.
Spoon on 200 ml (7 fl oz) of the
reserved stock.
3. Preheat the grill to hot.
4. Beat the fromage frais with the
mustard and sugar. Stir in the
breadcrumbs and half the Double
Gloucester cheese.
5. Spoon the mixture over the
vegetables and sprinkle the
remaining grated cheese on top.
Grill until brown and bubbling.
Freezing: not recommended

PARSNIPS WITH CARROT SAUCE

SERVES 4–6

250 g (8 oz) carrots, chopped
juice and finely grated zest of 1
 orange
150 g (5 oz) fromage frais
500 g (1 lb) young parsnips,
 peeled and quartered
 lengthways
25 g (1 oz) butter
2 tablespoons plain flour
150 ml (¼ pint) weak light stock
salt and pepper

1. Cook the carrots in boiling salted
water for 12–15 minutes until soft.
Drain and purée, with the orange
juice. Blend in the fromage frais and
orange zest.
2. Cook the parsnips in boiling
salted water for 8–10 minutes.
Drain, turn into a heated serving
dish and keep warm.
3. Meanwhile, melt the butter in a
pan. Stir in the flour and gradually
blend in the stock. Stir until
thickened and smooth.
4. Reduce the heat to low and stir in
the carrot purée and seasoning.
Heat through and spoon over the
parsnips. Serve hot.
Freezing: not recommended

Top *Parsnips with Carrot Sauce*,
below *Carrot and Leek Rarebit*

SWEET PEPPER AND OLIVE FLAN

SERVES 4–6

250 g (8 oz) ready-made
   shortcrust pastry
25 g (1 oz) butter
1 small onion, sliced
1 red pepper, sliced in rings
1 green pepper, sliced in rings
6 black olives, halved and stoned
2 eggs
200 g (7 oz) fromage frais
¼ teaspoon dried oregano
salt and pepper

1. Preheat the oven to Gas Mark
7/220°C/425°F.
2. Roll out the pastry and line a 20
cm (8-inch) flan tin. Line with
greaseproof paper and baking
beans, then bake blind for 10
minutes. Remove the lining and
cook for another 5 minutes.
3. Reduce the oven temperature to
Gas Mark 4/180°C/350°F.
4. Melt the butter in a pan on a low
heat and cook the onion and
peppers for 5 minutes. Arrange in
the pastry case with the olives.
5. Beat the eggs with the fromage
frais, oregano and seasoning.
Spoon over the vegetables and
bake for 35–40 minutes.
Freezing: recommended

POTATO BAKE

SERVES 4–6

750g (1½ lb) potatoes, cubed
   and boiled
25 g (1 oz) butter, plus extra for
   greasing
25 g (1 oz) Cheddar cheese,
   grated
1 small onion, chopped
3 tablespoons chopped fresh
   parsley
1 egg, separated, plus 1 egg yolk
175 g (6 oz) fromage frais
salt and pepper

1. Drain the potatoes and mash
with half the butter and the grated
Cheddar cheese.
2. Preheat the oven to Gas Mark
5/190°C/375°F.
3. Melt the remaining butter in a
pan on a low heat and cook the
onion for 2–3 minutes. Stir into the
potatoes, with the parsley.
4. Beat the 2 egg yolks, reserve a
little for glazing, and beat the
remainder into the potatoes. Add
the fromage frais and seasoning.
5. Whisk the egg white until stiff
and fold into the mixture. Spoon
into a greased 20 cm (8-inch), loose-
bottomed tin and bake for 45
minutes. Cool for 5 minutes,
remove from the tin and slice.
Freezing: not recommended

Top *Potato Bake*, below *Sweet
Pepper and Olive Flan*

FRUIT AND NUT FOOL

SERVES 4–5

75 g (3 oz) mixed dried fruit
grated zest and juice of ½ orange
750 g (1½ lb) cooking apples,
    peeled, cored and sliced
½ teaspoon ground cinnamon
2 cloves
a strip of lemon peel
1½ tablespoons clear honey
50 g (2 oz) chopped mixed nuts
250 g (8 oz) fromage frais

1. Put the dried fruit in a small dish and sprinkle on the orange zest and juice. Stand for 30 minutes.
2. Cook the apples with the cinnamon, cloves, lemon peel and honey in a tightly covered pan on a moderate heat for 10–12 minutes until soft and pulpy. Remove from the heat.
3. Uncover the apple mixture and leave to cool before discarding the cloves and lemon peel.
4. Purée the apples, then stir in the nuts and the dried fruit mixture. Gradually beat in the fromage frais.
5. Spoon the fool into serving dishes and chill for 1 hour.
Freezing: not recommended

STRAWBERRY CHEESE RINGS

SERVES 4–5

250 g (8 oz) strawberries, washed
    hulled and sliced
200 g (7 oz) 8% fat fromage frais
227 g (8 oz) carton of curd cheese
1 tablespoon icing sugar, sieved
1 tablespoon cornflour, sieved
1 tablespoon honey
1 tablespoon water

1. Crush 25 g (1 oz) of the strawberries and sieve them. Beat with the fromage frais, curd cheese, icing sugar and cornflour until light and fluffy.
2. Turn the cheese mixture into a piping bag fitted with a wide nozzle and pipe circles of the cheese onto small serving plates.
3. Warm the honey with the water and brush over the fruit to form a thin glaze.
4. Arrange the fruit in the cheese rings and serve immediately.

NOTE:
Kiwi fruit, mandarin segments or grapes can be used instead of strawberries.
Freezing: not recommended

Top *Strawberry Cheese Rings*,
below *Fruit and Nut Fool*

SLIMMERS' CHOCOLATE MOUSSE

SERVES 4–5

2×23 g sachet sugar-free
  drinking chocolate powder
1½ tablespoons caster sugar
3 tablespoons boiling water
11 g (0.4 oz) sachet of gelatine
6 tablespoons orange juice
375 g (12 oz) fromage frais
1 teaspoon clear honey
1 teaspoon grated chocolate

1. Blend the chocolate powder and sugar to a smooth paste with the boiling water.
2. Sprinkle the gelatine over the orange juice and stand for 3 minutes. Dissolve over a low heat and stir into the chocolate mixture.
3. Leave the chocolate mixture until lightly set, then beat until fluffy. Gradually add 300 g (10 oz) of the fromage frais, beating continuously.
4. Spoon the mousse into serving glasses or ramekins and chill until set.
5. Stir the honey into the remaining fromage frais and add a spoonful to each dessert. Top with a sprinkling of grated chocolate before serving.
Freezing: not recommended

MOULDED RASPBERRY CREAMS

SERVES 4

250 g (8 oz) raspberries, thawed if
  frozen
4 tablespoons orange juice
1 tablespoon honey
11 g (0.4 oz) sachet of gelatine
2 teaspoons brandy (optional)
300 g (10 oz) 8% fat fromage
  frais, plus a little extra

1. Reserve 12 raspberries, lightly crush the remainder and sieve into a pan. Discard the pips.
2. Stir the orange juice into the purée. Add the honey and stir on a low heat until dissolved.
3. Sprinkle the gelatine onto the mixture and dissolve over a low heat.
4. Remove the pan from the heat and cool for 5 minutes. Stir in the liqueur, if using, and the fromage frais.
5. Pour into wetted moulds, soufflé dishes or cut-down yogurt cartons and chill until set.
6. Unmould the creams onto small serving plates, add the reserved raspberries and a little extra fromage frais, if desired.
Freezing: recommended

Top *Moulded Raspberry Creams*, below *Slimmers' Chocolate Mousse*

LAYERED APRICOT CHEESECAKE

SERVES 6

125 g (4 oz) digestive biscuits, crushed
40 g (1½ oz) butter, melted
150 g (5 oz) dried apricots
125 ml (4 fl oz) orange juice
200 g (7 oz) 8% fat fromage frais
1 tablespoon caster sugar
2 eggs

1. Reserve a tablespoon of biscuit crumbs and mix the rest with the melted butter. Press into the base of a 15 cm (6-inch) loose-bottomed flan tin and chill for 30 minutes.
2. Put the apricots and orange juice in a small saucepan and bring to the boil. Cover and simmer for 5 minutes. Cool for 15 minutes.
3. Preheat the oven to Gas Mark 5/190°C/375°F.
4. Purée the apricots with their liquid and spread two-thirds in the prepared flan case.
5. Mix the remaining purée with the fromage frais, sugar and eggs and pour over the apricots.
6. Bake the cheesecake for 35–40 minutes. Cool for 5 minutes before removing from the tin and sprinkle with the reserved crumbs. Serve hot or cold.
Freezing: recommended

VEILED APPLE PUDDING

SERVES 4–6

625 g (1¼ lb) cooking apples, peeled, cored and sliced
250 g (8 oz) fromage frais
5 tablespoons clear honey
40 g (1½ oz) butter
125 g (4 oz) brown breadcrumbs
25 g (1 oz) brown sugar
213 g (7½ oz) can of blackcurrants in fruit juice
1 tablespoon cornflour
2 tablespoons water

1. Cook the apples with a little water in a covered pan until soft. Cool and purée with the fromage frais and half the honey.
2. Melt the butter in a pan and stir-fry the breadcrumbs for 2 minutes. Add the sugar and stir until crisp and brown.
3. Put the blackcurrants and juice and the remaining honey in a small saucepan. Blend the cornflour to a paste with the water and add.
4. On a moderate heat, bring the mixture to the boil, stirring. Cook for 2 minutes, then cool.
5. Layer the apples, blackcurrant mixture and crumbs in a dish, repeat, then chill for 1 hour.
Freezing: not recommended

Top *Layered Apricot Cheesecake*, below *Veiled Apple Pudding*

BREAD AND PINEAPPLE PUDDING

SERVES 4

25 g (1 oz) butter, plus a knob
227 g (8 oz) can of unsweetened
    pineapple pieces in natural
    juice
6 large slices of white bread
2 tablespoons clear honey
1 egg
200 g (7 oz) fromage frais
150 ml (¼ pint) milk

1. Preheat the oven to Gas Mark
4/180°C/350°F.
2. Use the knob of butter to grease
a medium-size baking dish and
spread the pineapple with a
tablespoonful of its juice in the
base.
3. Cut each slice of bread into four
squares and fit in a double layer
over the pineapple.
4. Melt the remaining butter with
the honey in a pan over low heat.
5. Whisk together the egg, fromage
frais and milk. Stir in the honey
mixture and pour over the bread.
6. Bake the pudding for 35–40
minutes until well-browned, and
serve hot.
Freezing: not recommended

BAKED COFFEE CUSTARD

SERVES 4–6

2 eggs
2½ tablespoons cornflour
1 teaspoon cocoa
3 tablespoons caster sugar
400 ml (14 fl oz) milk
1 tablespoon instant coffee
    powder
200 g (7 oz) fromage frais
1 banana, sliced

1. Preheat the oven to Gas Mark
4/180°C/350°F.
2. Beat the eggs with the cornflour,
cocoa and sugar.
3. Pour the milk into a saucepan and
add the coffee. Bring to boiling
point, then whisk into the egg
mixture.
4. Return the custard to the pan and
stir over a low heat until thickened
and smooth. Remove from the
heat.
5. Cool the custard for 5 minutes,
then whisk in the fromage frais and
pour into a baking dish. Bake for
30–35 minutes, until lightly set. Add
a border of sliced banana and serve
hot.
Freezing: not recommended

Top *Bread and Pineapple Pudding*,
below *Baked Coffee Custard*

SPICED PANCAKES

SERVES 4–6

100 g (3½ oz) plain flour, sifted
a good pinch of salt
1 egg
275 ml (9 fl oz) milk
65 g (2½ oz) butter, melted
200 g (7 oz) fromage frais
125 g (4 oz) cream cheese
1 teaspoon ground cinnamon
1½ teaspoons cornflour
50 g (2 oz) seedless raisins
1 large orange

1. Sift the flour with the salt. Beat the egg and milk and stir in a tablespoon of the butter. Add the liquids to the flour mixture and whisk until smooth and creamy.
2. Coat a heavy-based pan with a film of melted butter and place on a moderate heat. When hot, swirl on 2 tablespoons of batter and cook for 1–2 minutes until set. Turn and brown the second side.
3. Cook the remaining pancakes.
4. Beat the fromage frais, cream cheese, cinnamon and cornflour until smooth. Add the raisins and grate in the zest from the orange.
5. Spoon the mixture onto the pancakes and fold up into neat parcels, tucking in the sides to enclose the filling.
6. Peel and slice the orange.
7. Heat half the butter in a pan and fry the pancake, folded side down, for 1 minute. Turn and cook for 1 minute more, adding a little butter. Serve hot with the orange.
Freezing: not recommended

COCONUT SPONGE

SERVES 4–6

3 eggs, separated
finely grated zest and juice of 1 lemon
200 ml (7 fl oz) milk
125 g (4 oz) fromage frais
100 g (3½ oz) caster sugar
a good pinch of salt
50 g (2 oz) plain flour
50 g (2 oz) desiccated coconut
butter for greasing

1. Preheat the oven to Gas Mark 4/180°C/350°F.
2. Whisk the egg yolks with the lemon zest and juice, milk and fromage frais. Gradually whisk in the sugar, salt and flour.
3. Reserve a little coconut and stir the rest into the mixture.
4. Whisk the egg whites until stiff peaks form. With a metal spoon, fold them into the egg mixture.
5. Turn the pudding into a greased 1-litre (1¾-pint) baking dish. Sprinkle with the reserved coconut.
6. Bake for 30–35 minutes.
Freezing: not recommended

Top *Spiced Pancakes*, below *Coconut Sponge*

EASY IDEAS FOR FROMAGE FRAIS

* To make a delicious dip, dilute a 600 ml (1 pint) packet soup, such as French onion, with 125 ml (4 fl oz) of boiling water, stir to a paste, leave till cold, then mix with 500 g (1 lb) of fromage frais

* Blend fromage frais with canned fish to make either a dip or a sandwich filling

* Make into a sandwich filling with cucumber, chicken, pepper and walnuts

* Blend with fresh soft fruit to make a quick dessert

* Layer between sponges and fruit to make quick individual trifles, adding custard if you wish

* Add to porridge or muesli at breakfast

* Use as a low-fat topping on fruit pies and other desserts

* Stir into casseroles or soups instead of cream

* Serve with soft summer fruit instead of whipped cream

* Blend in a little cornflour and use it for piping decorations on cakes and sweets, instead of cream

* Add it to mayonnaise to make a lighter dressing

* Stir into cheese sauce for added smoothness

* Try with warm scones or croissants and jam